11/13 6x 8/16

DISCARD

 W9-CEI-148

DISCARD

DATE DUE

FEB 0 3 2007 FEB 2 6 2007		
GAYLORD		PRINTED IN U.S.A.

DISCARD

DEC 2 2006

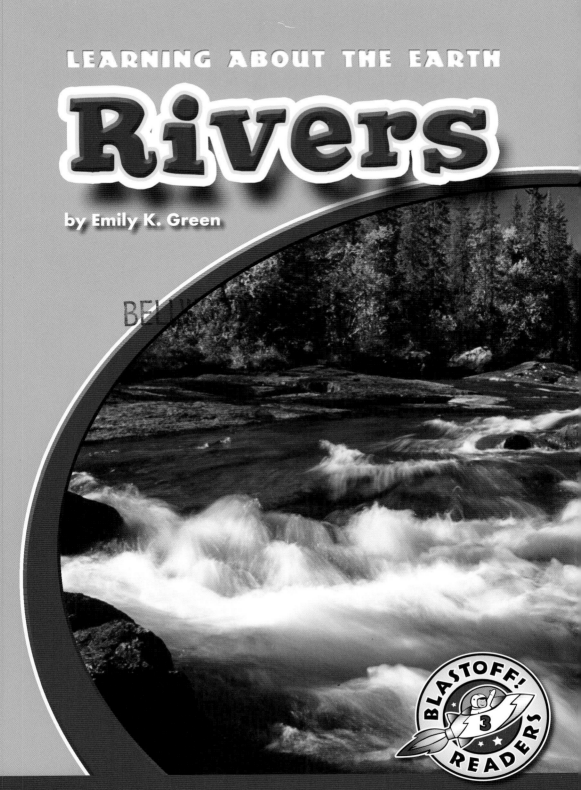

LEARNING ABOUT THE EARTH

Rivers

by Emily K. Green

BELLWETHER MEDIA · MINNEAPOLIS, MN

BLASTOFF!
3
READERS

Note to Librarians, Teachers, and Parents:

Blastoff! Readers are carefully developed by literacy experts and combine standards-based content with developmentally appropriate text.

Level 1 provides the most support through repetition of high-frequency words, light text, predictable sentence patterns, and strong visual support.

Level 2 offers early readers a bit more challenge through varied simple sentences, increased text load, and less repetition of high-frequency words.

Level 3 advances early-fluent readers toward fluency through increased text and concept load, less reliance on visuals, longer sentences, and more literary language.

Whichever book is right for your reader, Blastoff! Readers are the perfect books to build confidence and encourage a love of reading that will last a lifetime!

This edition first published in 2007 by Bellwether Media.

No part of this publication may be reproduced in whole or in part without written permission of the publisher. For information regarding permission, write to Bellwether Media Inc., Attention: Permissions Department, Post Office Box 1C, Minnetonka, MN 55345-9998.

Library of Congress Cataloging-in-Publication Data
Green, Emily K., 1966–
  Rivers / by Emily K. Green.
    p. cm. — (Blastoff! readers) (Learning about the Earth)
Summary: "Simple text and supportive images introduce beginning readers to the physical characteristics of rivers."
  Includes bibliographical references and index.
  ISBN-10: 1-60014-040-8 (hardcover : alk. paper)
  ISBN-13: 978-1-60014-040-2 (hardcover : alk. paper)
  1. Rivers—Juvenile literature. I. Title. II. Series.

GB1203.8G737 2007
551.48'3—dc22   2006000608

Text copyright © 2007 by Bellwether Media.
Printed in the United States of America.

Table of Contents

A river is water that makes a path across the land. Rivers flow through cities and towns.

Rivers flow through forests and **farmland**.

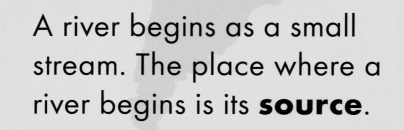

A river begins as a small stream. The place where a river begins is its **source**.

The stream gets wider as it flows away from its source. A small stream runs into a bigger one. Rain adds more water. The stream becomes a river.

Rivers always flow **downhill**.
This river is flowing quickly down
a steep slope. When water rushes
over rocks it makes **rapids**.

This river is flowing slowly down a gentle slope.

Some rivers end by flowing into another river or a lake.

Many rivers end by flowing into the ocean. The end of a river is its **mouth**.

The movement of water is the **current**. Moving water wears away the earth.

Over time, a river can make a deep **canyon**.

The land underneath the river is the **riverbed**. A waterfall is a place where the riverbed drops off steeply.

The sides of the river are the **banks**.

Too much rain can cause a **flood**. Floods happen when water spills over the banks of a river.

People build walls
called **levees** to
stop floods.

Fish live in rivers.

Sometimes fish swim against the current. This **salmon** is trying to get **upstream** to lay its eggs.

Rivers carry fresh water.
Fresh water is not salty.

Boats carry people and **goods** from one place to another along the river. Rivers are like highways made of water.

Glossary

bank—the edge of the river

canyon—a place where a river cuts into rock

current—the movement of the water

downhill—moving from a higher place toward a lower place

farmland—land where people grow plants for food

flood—when water rises and overflows the banks of a river

goods—things that people use

levee—a wall that people build to keep a river from overflowing

mouth—the place where a river ends; rivers end by flowing into a bigger body of water like a lake or an ocean.

rapids—water flowing quickly over rocks

riverbed—the land underneath the river

salmon—a fish that is born in a river; salmon swim back to the place they were born to lay their eggs.

source—the start of a river

upstream—the direction towards the source of a river; against the current

To Learn More

AT THE LIBRARY

Bour, Laura. *The River*. New York: Scholastic, 1993.

Browne, Michael Dennis. *Give Her the River: A Father's Wish for His Daughter*. New York: Atheneum Books, 2004.

Esbaum, Jill. *Ste-e-e-amboat A'Comin'*. New York: Farrar, Strauss and Giroux, 2005.

LaMarche, Jim. *The Raft*. New York, Harper Trophy, 2002.

Locker, Thomas. *Where the River Begins*. New York: Dial Books, 1984.

Singer, Marilyn. *Monday on the Mississippi*. New York: Henry Holt, 2005.

ON THE WEB

Learning more about rivers is as easy as 1, 2, 3.

1. Go to www.factsurfer.com

2. Enter "rivers" into search box.

3. Click the "Surf" button and you will see a list of related web sites.

With factsurfer.com, finding more information is just a click away.

Index